MW01017125

Four Phases of Women's Careers

Becoming Gender Bilingual

Avivah Wittenberg-Cox

© 2016

Published by 20-first Publishers

ISBN: 978-0-9935463-0-3

www.20-first.com

Are Men and Women Different?

☐ Yes

☐ No

If YES proceed to Question 2
If NO. Stop reading. (Waste of time)

Has
Today's
WORK
WORLD
been
designed
by
MEN
for
MEN

What do you call

SUCCESS

Does it look like this?...

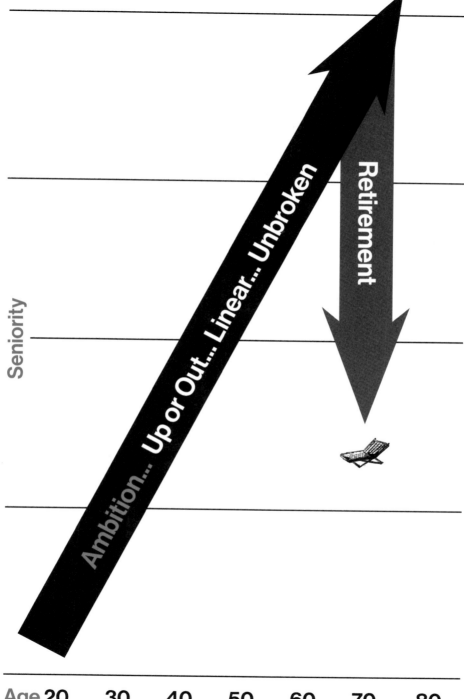

Seniority

Ambition... Up or Out... Linear... Unbroken

Retirement

Age 20   30   40   50   60   70   80

If yes... that doesn't work for women

(Not to mention most of Gen Y, Z...)

o

If NO, BRAVO you're ahead of the curve

Women have
FO

UR

key career phases...

20s

Ambition

30s

Culture Shock

40s
Re-Acceleration

50+
Self-
Actualisation

(And with a 100-year life, there will soon be four more)

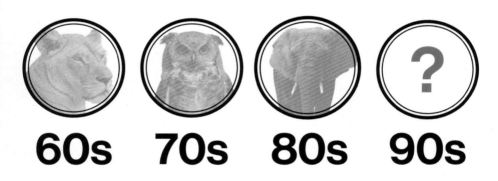

60s   70s   80s   90s

(But that's for another book...)

for now...

20s
Ambition

Women	Companies
Convinced gender issues are obsolete	**Recruiting gender balanced teams**
Super educated	No differences
Super ambitious	**Solved it!**
Gonna have it all!	

'This is fun'   'This is fun'

30s
Culture Shock

Women	Companies
Delay personal choices then SUDDENLY...	**Identify high-potential talent**
get married, have a kid, maybe 2 (in France maybe 3)	Big jobs to test
	International mobility
'I QUIT'	'Her choice'

40s
Re-Accelerate

Women		Companies
Kids in school		She fell off hi-po list
Breathing again		Never got back on
Ready for growth		Doesn't have key experience
Guy next door got promoted		

'Start my own biz'

'Where have all the women gone?'

50s
Self-Actualisation

Women	Companies
The very best career years	**Oh boy, no women**
think...	**Doesn't look good**
Mary Barra	**Can we find one for the board?**
Christine Lagarde	
Angela Merkel	
Indra Nooyi	
Virginia Rometty	
etc...	
'I'm a non-exec director'	'We're gender fatigued'

Is your career model?

A LADDER
(uniform)

OR A LATTICE
(flexibility, for ALL)

P.S. This ain't just a women's issue...

Just the future of work for...

Men
Women
Gen Y & Z
Seniors
Your kids
YOU!

**getting women
to adapt to the world
of work...**

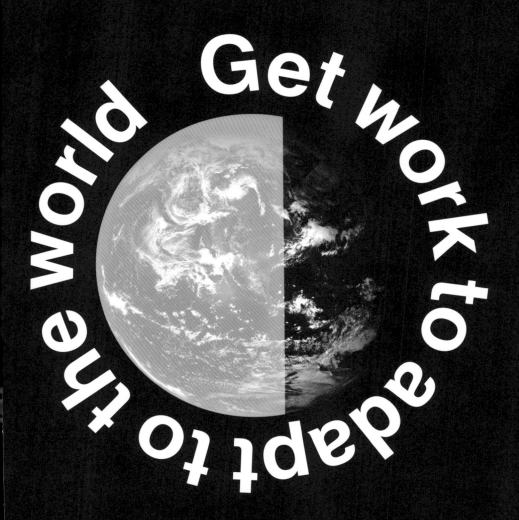

Get work to adapt to the world

(Much easier...)

Does your company manage the

WH

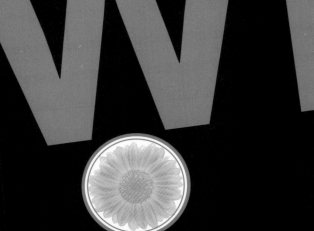

20s

Identify hi-po early

International
mobility early

Mentor

Go fast

30s

Keep on hi-po lists

Gender neutralise
parental leave

**Allow plateaux/
sabbaticals/returns**

Be flexible

Sponsor

CYCLE?

40s	50+
Develop	**Promote balanced leadership styles**
Take chances	Visibly gender balance the top
Promote, international mobility, big jobs	**Create role models**
Focus on balance	Promote
Re-accelerate	

The world is waiting
Flex your mind

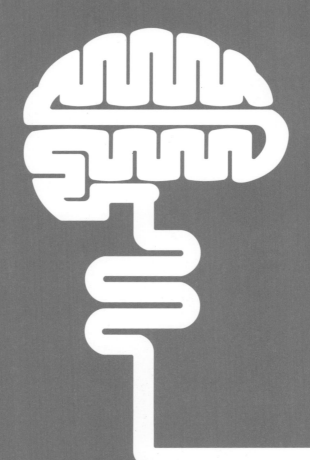

Then flex your systems

Do your managers get it?

Do they allow, support, enable, and applaud gender bilingual career management?

Gender Bilingual

The management competency that equips all managers, male and female, to understand the differences between genders in order to be able to effectively recruit, retain and develop 100% of the talent pool, and to be able to understand, connect and communicate with 100% of customers, end-users and stakeholders.

Balanced Leadership

Range of different kinds of personalities, behaviours and strengths in leadership that include the spectrum from feminine to masculine, as opposed to the preponderance of a single, usually male style, often of a single (home country) nationality and/ or job function.

Role Models

Leaders (male AND female) who are aspirational to 100% of the talent pool - and reflect it. So, not women that have had to become men in order to succeed, nor managers who ignore people's personal lives and whole selves.

Lattice vs Ladder

Career ladders are homogeneous, single path career patterns, that often stick within single functions or divisions and are usually based on up or out decisions. Career lattices recognise that learning is life long and can happen across functions, areas and levels. Flexibility, variety and adaptability are the name of the game, not status, promotion and power.

Parental Leave

Key career management issue for women is to gender neutralise traditional gender roles. One of the biggest shifts will be shifting from maternity leave to parental leave, and ensuring that men take it (and feel encouraged to take it). That will truly level the playing field.

International Mobility

To ensure that mobile talent is gender balanced, start early. Get people moving in their 20s, be sensitive about moving them in their 30s (to countries where household help is readily available, for example), and then accelerate mobility in the 50+.

Mentoring vs Sponsoring

Mentoring is informal advice from a senior manager. Sponsoring is where leaders are accountable for the career development of key talent.

And the ladies lived happily ever after...

(And the men did too)

Author: Avivah Wittenberg-Cox
Designer: Wayne Ford

www.20-first.com